Handprint Art

Handprint People

By
Henu
Mehtani

Crabtree Publishing Company
www.crabtreebooks.com

Crabtree Publishing Company
www.crabtreebooks.com
1-800-387-7650

616 Welland Ave.
St. Catharines, ON
L2M 5V6

PMB 59051, 350 Fifth Ave.
59th Floor,
New York, NY 10118

Published in 2017 by CRABTREE PUBLISHING COMPANY.

Author: Henu Mehtani

Illustrator: Henu Mehtani

Editorial director: Felicia Law

Project Coordinator: , Kathy Middleton

Editors: Saranne Taylor, Petrice Custance

Proofreader: Wendy Scavuzzo

Prepress technician: Tammy McGarr

Print coordinator: Katherine Berti

Art and Illustrations: Copyright © 2015
Henu Studio Pvt. Ltd.
All rights reserved
www.henustudio.com

Edition copyright © 2015 BrambleKids Ltd

Printed in Hong Kong/012017/BK20161024

Library and Archives Canada Cataloguing in Publication

Mehtani, Henu, author
    Handprint people / Henu Mehtani.

(Handprint art)
ISBN 978-0-7787-3111-5 (hardback).--
ISBN 978-0-7787-3124-5 (paperback)

    1. Finger painting--Juvenile literature. 2. Human beings in art--Juvenile literature. 3. Painting--Technique--Juvenile literature. 4. Handicraft for children--Juvenile literature. I. Title.

ND2490.M447 2016   j751.4'9   C2016-906648-7

Library of Congress Cataloging-in Publication Data

Names: Mehtani, Henu, author.
Title: Handprint people / Henu Mehtani.
Description: New York : Crabtree Publishing, 2017. |
  Series: Handprint art |
  Includes index. | Audience: Ages 5-8. | Audience: K to grade 3.
Identifiers: LCCN 2016046756|
  ISBN 9780778731115 (hardcover : alk. paper) |
  ISBN 9780778731245 (pbk. : alk. paper)
Subjects: LCSH: Art--Technique--Juvenile literature. | Human beings in art--Juvenile literature. | Fingerprints in art--Juvenile literature.
Classification: LCC N7433 .M357 2017 | DDC 700/.453--dc23
LC record available at https://lccn.loc.gov/2016046756

Contents

You will need

- Drawing paper or a sketch book
- Tempera paints. The more colors the better!
- Paintbrushes. Try different sizes, such as a round brush, a thin brush, and a flat brush.
- Apron and cloths for keeping clean
- Your own hands!

Tips

- Work on the background of your artwork before you make your handprint people. You can either copy the backgrounds from this book, or you can be creative and design your own!
- Remember to allow the paint to dry between layers. Be sure to wash your hands before switching to a new color.

Experiment

- Try using different colors than the colors listed in the book. Be creative!
- Once you have practiced on paper, you can try to make pictures and designs on a T-shirt or pillow case. Just use fabric paints instead!

Juggler ... tossing balls

What to do

- Paint a circle on your hand for the head. Paint your fingers blue. Print your hand upside down, with a space between your closed fingers to make the legs.

- Paint your fingertips different colors to print the shirt.

- Use fingerprints to make the hair, hands, and ears.

- Use a red fingerprint for the nose, yellow fingerprints for the skirt, and colorful fingerprints for the balls.

- Use a thin brush to paint the hat, face, collar, and feet.

Trapeze artist ... swinging high

What to do

- Paint your hand yellow with colorful stripes in a V-shape. Print with a space between your closed fingers to make the legs.

- Use yellow fingers to print the arms, and blue fingerprints for the feet.

- Paint your fingertips to make the face, hands, and ears. Use a thumbprint for the hair.

- Use a fine brush to paint the **trapeze,** eyes, and mouth.

Stiltwalker ... so tall

What to do

- Paint your hand purple with red patches. Print upside down with a space between your closed fingers for the legs.

- Print your thumb again to make the second arm. Print your fingers again to make the legs longer.

- Use blue fingerprints to decorate the clothes, purple fingerprints to make the hat, and black fingerprints for the **stilts**.

- Use a fine brush to paint the hands and face.

Cowboy ... on your horse

What to do

- Paint your hand blue with a gray stripe across the bottom of your fingers. Print your hand upside down with your fingers closed.

- Print your thumb again to make the other arm. Print your fingers again to finish the legs.

- Use gray fingerprints for the gun **holsters**, hair, shoes, and buttons. Use different shades of brown fingerprints to make the hat and guns.

- Use a fine brush to paint the scarf, face, hands, and to add a stripe on the hat.

Wizard ...
with magical powers

What to do

- Paint your whole hand blue and print it upside down.

- Print your thumb again to make the second arm. Print your fingers again to finish the bottom of the wizard's **cloak**.

- Use a fine brush to paint the face, hands, and wand.

- Use gray fingerprints for the beard, blue and red for the hat, and yellow to decorate the cloak.

- Use a yellow thumbprint, then a smaller orange thumbprint to make the flash of light on the wand.

8

Astronaut ... on the Moon

What to do

● Paint a gray circle on your palm and print. Then paint your whole hand gray and print it upside down under the circle, with a space between your closed fingers for the legs.

● Print your little finger to make the second arm. Use gray thumbprints to make the boots.

● Use a fine brush to paint the gray backpack, the face, and the white front **panel**. Use colorful fingerprints to make the **controls**.

Baby ... time for tea

What to do

- Paint a circle on your palm and print it to make the head. Paint your whole palm yellow with an orange stripe in the middle. Print it upside down under the circle.

- Use fingerprints to make the arms, ears, and hair.

- Use blue fingerprints to make the legs, red fingerprints for the shoes, and a purple fingerprint for the lollipop.

- Use a fine brush to paint the bib, lollipop stick, and face.

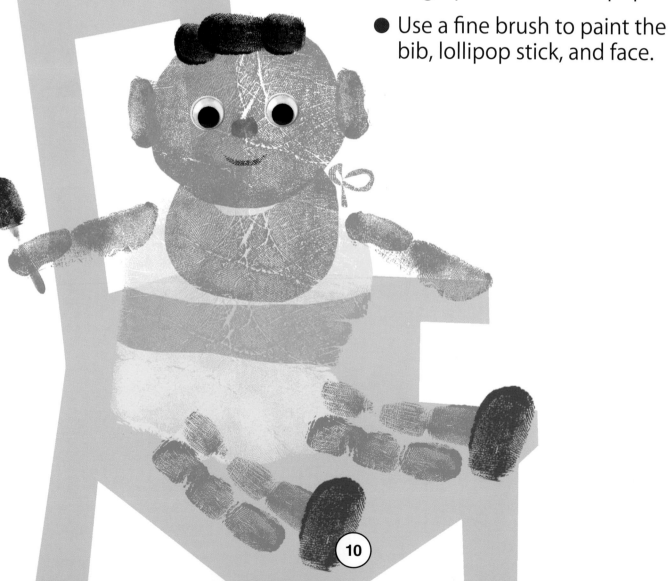

Chef ...
what's for supper?

What to do

● Paint your whole hand light blue and print it upside down. Use fingerprints to fill in the chef's **apron**. Print your little finger again to make the second arm.

● Paint a circle on your palm to print the head. Use light blue fingerprints to make the chef's hat.

● Use fingerprints to make the hair, ears, and hands.

● Use a fine brush to paint the serving dish, jacket decorations, and face.

Ballerina ...
dance across the stage

What to do

- Paint your palm pink and print it upside down to make the skirt.

- Use two pink thumbprints to make the ballerina's body. Use small pink fingerprints to make the bottom of the skirt.

- Use your fingertips to print the ballerina's head, arms, legs, shoes, and hair.

- Use a fine brush to paint the hair ribbon, the dots on the dress, and the face.

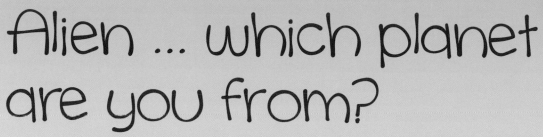

Alien ... which planet are you from?

14

What to do

- Paint a green circle on your palm and print it. Paint your whole palm green. Print it upside down below the circle.

- Use green fingers to make the **antennae**, ears, arms, legs, and feet.

- Use a fine brush to paint on the face.

- Experiment with different faces and poses for your alien!

What to do

- Paint your palm with a square and print it. Paint your whole palm, your thumb, and your little finger blue and print it upside down below the square.

- Paint your fingers dark red and print the legs. Use fingerprints for the hands, ears, and hair. Use black thumbprints to make the boots.

- Use a fine brush to paint the face, wooden club, and decorate the clothes.

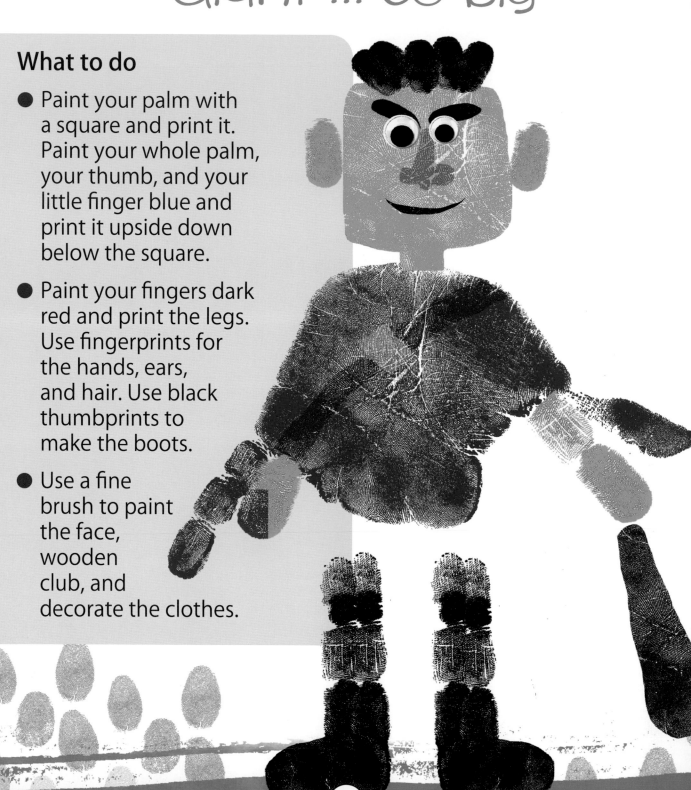

Pirate ... up to no good

What to do

- Paint your whole hand black. Print it upside down.

- Paint your palm with a circle. Print over your handprint for the face. Use the same color fingerprint to make the hand.

- Use a fine brush to paint on the hat, headscarf, black hair, wooden leg, and face.

- Decorate the hair with colorful fingerprints.

Clown ... on his unicycle

What to do

- Paint a circle on the top of your palm, and a colorful strip below it. Print your palm.

- Paint your finger with different colors to print the arms and legs.

- Use fingerprints to make the ears, hands, and hair. Use red fingerprints for the nose, and blue fingerprints for the feet.

- For the unicycle, use a gray fingerprint for the seat, purple fingerprints for the **frame**, and black fingerprints for the wheel.

- Use a thin brush to paint the rest of the unicycle, and the face.

Fairy ... with her wand

What to do

- Paint a circle on your palm and print it. Paint your whole hand pink. Print it upside down below the circle. Use fingerprints to make the fairy's skirt.

- Use fingerprints to make the arms, legs, and hair. Use red fingerprints for the shoes, and white for the buttons.

- Use a fine brush to paint the wings, wand, headband, and face. Decorate the wings with fingerprints.

Snowman ... happy in the cold

What to do

- Paint a small white circle on your palm and print it. Paint a bigger circle. Print it below the small circle. Repeat with an even bigger circle.

- Use a pink fingerprint for the nose. Use red, yellow, and blue fingerprints to make the hat, blue for the scarf, and gray for the buttons.

- Use a fine brush to paint the eyes, mouth, and arms. Paint white dots for the button holes.

The king and queen ... bow

What to do

- Paint your hand red for the king's cloak. Print it upside down. Use your fingerprints again to make the cloak longer. Repeat with blue paint to make the queen's cloak.

- Paint a circle on your palm. Print it above the red cloak to make the king's head. Repeat to make the queen's head.

22

- Use fingerprints to make hair, ears, and hands. Use yellow fingerprints for the crowns and jewelry. Decorate the clothes with colorful fingerprints.

- Use a fine brush to paint on the rest of the jewelry, the king's **staff**, and the king's and queen's faces.

Waiters ... how can I help you?

What to do

- Paint your fingers black. Print them with a space between your closed fingers to make the legs. Use black fingerprints for the feet.

- Paint the bottom of your palm white. Print it upside down on top of the legs to make the waiter's apron. Paint your palm black with a white U-shaped part on the bottom of your palm. Print it upside down to make the body.

- Paint a circle on your palm. Print it to make the waiter's head.

- Use fingerprints to make the hair, ears, and hands. Paint your fingers white for the arms. Use yellow fingerprints for the wine.

- Use a fine brush to paint the bow tie, wine glasses, and face.

Mom and Dad ... in a photo

What to do

- Paint a circle on your palm. Print twice for the heads.

- Paint your palm, thumb, and little finger green, and your other fingers orange. Print upside down under one circle to make the mother's body. Repeat with different colors to make the father's body.

- Use fingerprints to make the hair, ears, and hands.

- Use a fine brush to paint the tie, bags, earrings, glasses, and faces. Paint a picture frame around the mother and father.

Girl ... on roller skates

What to do

- Paint your palm, thumb, and little finger pink with purple stripes. Print upside down for the body.

- Use a thumbprint for the face. Use fingerprints to make the hands and hair.

- Use blue fingerprints for the legs, and red fingerprints to make the ribbons and roller skates.

- Use a fine brush to paint the face, the wheels, and the laces on the skates.

28

Grandparents ... going for a walk

What to do

- Paint a circle on your palm. Print it twice to make the heads.

- Paint your palm and thumb the colors you've chosen for grandpa's clothes. Paint your fingers the color of his pants. Print your hand upside down under the circle. Repeat with different colors to make grandma's clothes.

- Use fingerprints to make the hat, hair, moustache, ears, and hands.

- Use a fine brush to paint the cane, glasses, necklace, and faces.

Swimmer ... diving in the waves

What to do

- Paint a small circle on your palm. Make half of it red for the bathing cap. Print the circle just above the water to make the head.

- Paint your palm, and add a strip of purple at the top. Print above the head of the swimmer to make the body.

- Use fingerprints to make the arms, legs, ears, and feet.

- Use a fine brush to paint the face and **goggles**.

Hula dancer ...
in a grass skirt

- Paint a circle on your palm and print for the head. Paint your whole palm, thumb, and little finger the same color. Print upside down under the circle to make the body and arms.

- Paint your fingertips green and print to make the skirt.

- Use fingerprints to make the hair and legs.

- Use blue thumbprints for the bikini top, and pink and white fingerprints for the flowers around the dancer's neck, head, and arms.

- Use a fine brush to paint the face.

Glossary

antennae Threadlike feelers on the head of an insect

apron An item worn on the front of the body that ties around the waist with strings. It is usually worn to protect clothing during cooking

cloak An item worn over clothing, similar to a cape

controls Knobs buttons or keys used to control a machine

goggles A type of glasses worn to protect the eyes from water, light, dust, or dangerous chemicals

holsters Cases used to hold a gun, usually worn on a belt

panel A rectangular plate that usually holds the control buttons

staff A rod carried by royalty or by someone in a position of power

stilts Tall poles that attach to the feet and allow the user to walk above the ground

trapeze A device used by acrobats. A handlebar is connected to two ropes that hang down from a high ceiling, allowing the acrobat to swing through the air

Learning more

Books

Corfee, Stephanie. *Paint Lab for Kids: 52 Creative Adventures in Painting and Mixed Media for Budding Artists of All Ages.* Quarry Books, 2015.

Levy, Barbara Soloff. *How to Draw People.* Dover Publications, 2002.

Websites

Visit this site for tons of handprint craft ideas: **www.dltk-kids.com/type/handprint.htm**

Check out this fun online painting machine: **www.nga.gov/content/ngaweb/education/kids/kids-brushster.html**